Collins

Learn to Paint

Vibrant
Watercolours

Haze

Dedication
To my vibrant son Sean

First published in 2000, this edition published in **2008** by
Collins, an imprint of
HarperCollinsPublishers
77-85 Fulham Palace Road
Hammersmith
London W6 8JB

The Collins website address is www.**collins**.co.uk

Collins is a registered trademark of HarperCollins Publishers Ltd.

11 10 09 08
4 3 2

© Hazel Soan 2000

Hazel Soan asserts the moral right to be identified as the author of this work.

A catalogue record for this book is available from the British Library

Editor: Geraldine Christy
Layout Designer: Liz Brown
Photographer: Laura Wickenden

ISBN-13 978 0 00 719399 8

Colour reproduction by Colourscan, Singapore
Printed and bound by Printing Express, Hong Kong

Previous page: **Nothing is Black & White** 18 x 15 cm (7 x 6 in)
This page: **The Colour of Speed** 30 x 41 cm (12 x 16 in)
Opposite: **Grape Vine, Warden Abbey Vineyard** 23 x 30 cm (9 x 12 in)

Contents

Portrait of an Artist

Hazel Soan was born in Surrey and began painting prolifically as a young teenager. At art college she realized that her passion in life was painting, and learning about living artists gave her the courage to believe she could earn a living from her art work. Glimpsing a confidential report at college proved the catalyst she needed. It read, 'Hazel has schoolgirl enthusiasm and romantic ideals about being an artist.' Rising

◀ Hazel Soan painting in her London garden.

to the challenge she arranged her first exhibition soon after graduating. She sold nothing, but, undaunted, she rented a studio and continued to paint in between working behind the bar at a local pub. One of the patrons suggested a gallery in London she should approach and soon she had another exhibition on the horizon. This time her watercolours sold out within the first hour. Her career was launched.

Since then Hazel has exhibited widely and has over 20 one-woman shows to her credit. She travels avidly for the source of her paintings. For the last few years Africa has held her passion – the people, animals and landscape never cease to enthral her.

Her paintings, both oils and watercolours, are collected by private and corporate buyers throughout the world. Several international hotels display her work and Sotheby's and Christie's have auctioned her paintings.

Sharing her passion

Hazel also enjoys writing. She wants others to experience the thrill of painting and encourages people to shed their fears and paint with enthusiasm. She contributes regularly to art magazines and has published two previous instructional books – *Collins Watercolour Flower Painting Workshop* and *The Encyclopaedia of Landscape Watercolour Techniques*.

Hazel also enjoys the medium of television broadcasting, which allows her to communicate her passion for art to a wider audience. She first appeared on television in 1978, talking about her work at the Royal Academy Summer Show for the BBC. Since then she has filmed two series of *Splash of Colour* for Anglia TV. She has been a guest on *Wish You Were Here* and *The Great Picture Chase* with David Gower for the BBC. Hazel has been interviewed for radio, magazines and newspapers many times, and her biography is published in *Artists' Stories*.

Driven by a strong and cheerful faith in God, Hazel hopes that her paintings enhance

▲ **Out of the Blue**
53 x 43 cm (21 x 17 in)

other people's lives. She believes that we all have the seed of creativity invested within us by our creator, and that all you need to be able to paint is the desire to paint.

Hazel lives through her eyes, seeing potential paintings everywhere. Despite her success and the thousands of pictures she has produced, she still feels trepidation before a piece of white paper. It is this constant challenge and the desire to make images of what excites her visually that keeps her paintings vibrant.

Vibrant Watercolours

Imagine mouthwatering colours skimming across the textured white paper, with deep mysterious darks dissolving softly into radiant lights. Vibrant watercolours are those that sing out from the page. They make you feel good, they seduce you with their bold impact and wonderful techniques. They are a delight to behold and a joy for the artist to paint.

How do you paint vibrant watercolours? How do you prevent your paintings from becoming lacklustre or overworked? The secret is in knowing what watercolour can do, and having the confidence to use that knowledge. The best way to gain confidence is to practise, but few people actually have enough spare time to do so. The aim of this book is to short cut your practice time and suggest ways in which you can make your own paintings vibrant.

The right approach

When you are learning to use watercolours you can sometimes try so hard that your paintings are filled with frustration and overworking, losing their liveliness. However, there are aids to follow that will help you make your paintings vibrant. By choosing a subject you really like and are

▲ **This is My Town**
43 x 56 cm (17 x 22 in)
Watercolour, with its rainbow of pigments, spontaneous brushwork and the immediacy of translucent washes, is the perfect medium for creating lively, animated paintings.

6

▼ Decked in Scarlet
76 x 56 cm (30 x 22 in)
One of the most exciting qualities of watercolour is its power to suggest detail without actually painting it. Wet-in-wet washes create ambiguity, brush strokes create energy and an understated approach draws the viewer into the painting.

interested in, allowing yourself to be relaxed about the painting process, and genuinely enjoying mixing and laying those delicious colours, there is every chance that you can create a successful watercolour. Look hard before painting, examine the subject as if seeing it for the first time, and put aside any preconceptions of how you think something must look.

What is your goal?

Most beginners are only too happy to achieve some form of likeness to their chosen subject. But this, though admirable, is not your only goal, You want to paint something with that little bit extra, a

painting that goes beyond straight reproduction. Perhaps what really attracts you to paint a subject is actually not the subject itself, but the way the light falls upon it, or the arrangement of shapes. That attraction or inspiration is what you want your painting to be about.

Striking a chord

Sometimes when you strike a slightly off-beat chord visually you create a watercolour that is vibrant. Even a mundane object like a pair of old boots can make an exciting painting. If you approach an age-old theme in a refreshingly different way the viewer is jolted into a response, momentarily seeing with your eyes and feeling your passion.

When something is understated, or slightly ambiguous, it often attracts attention; in order to see it clearly the viewer has to get involved, and is consequently drawn into the picture.

Know-how

Technical ability is not a prerequisite for a vibrant watercolour. However, becoming familiar with colours and tones and learning to apply paint effectively to paper will help you to express your interest in the subject with confidence, and enable you to achieve the lively, vibrant watercolours you seek. This book shows the main watercolour techniques and gives special attention to brush strokes and laying paint as well as examining the thought behind the painting.

Step-by-step demonstrations guide you through the process of building up a watercolour, and encourage you to convey your inspiration and passion in vibrant watercolours of your own. Here is a world longing to be explored. Have fun!

Materials and Equipment

You need very few materials to make effective watercolour paintings. The less you have to carry and think about the more likely you are to succeed in making your paintings work.

The only materials you require are a brush, a paintbox or a few colours and a palette, paper, water and a rag. Depending on the size at which you choose to work, these items can fit into a small light bag or a large pocket.

As you gain confidence you will inevitably want to try out more colours and different shaped or sized brushes. You will want to paint larger. But I recommend that you work with minimum equipment to start with and build up more as you find the need.

Brushes

The most important piece of equipment is the brush. It is the extension of your hand and eye when painting, so it must be as sensitive and versatile as you. It is the one item you should not economize on. The best brushes are made of pure sable. A good brush holds ample paint between the hairs in the body of the brush, yet even in the largest sizes has a tip capable of painting fine detail. Buy a size 7 round brush (Daler-Rowney Diana or Series 40 are good quality) made of Kolinsky sable and see how broad a wash you can achieve and how fine a line you can draw with the same brush. If you plan to work small a size 5 will do, and if you work larger choose a size 10 or 12. Check the quality of the tip when you buy the brush.

You can add to your brush collection flat brushes for broad washes and different brush marks, and big cheap mops for distributing paint on a large scale.

Paints

Watercolour paint is available in tubes or pans. In the pans it is in solid form and in the tubes it is thick and fluid. For small sketches and outdoor work a paintbox with pans of colour is the most convenient. For washes and larger work where you require a greater quantity of colour you will need to use paint from tubes. A basic palette of colours supplemented with tubes for the colours you use most often is a perfect working combination.

The standard paintbox has a palette of two opening leaves for colour mixing. You may find you need more space than this, or you may want to mix larger pools of colour. A porcelain palette with several compartments is therefore a useful addition.

Manufacturers make two grades of colours. Artists' colours are made with ground pigments and will create the most vibrant colours and tonal variations. Student colours are made with cheaper pigments, so are less intense, but also less expensive to buy. If cost is an issue student colours are fine for learning. When you have discovered the colours you prefer to use it is worthwhile upgrading to better-quality paints.

▲ Do not confuse yourself with too much equipment. One brush, three colours (a red, a yellow and a blue), some water and some paper is all you really need.

► Maybe I am a romantic, but I find even the painting paraphernalia of palettes, brushes and tubes of paint utterly mouthwatering.

▼ As a basic rule you need to have a warm and cool version of each of the primary colours (blue, red, yellow) and some earth colours.

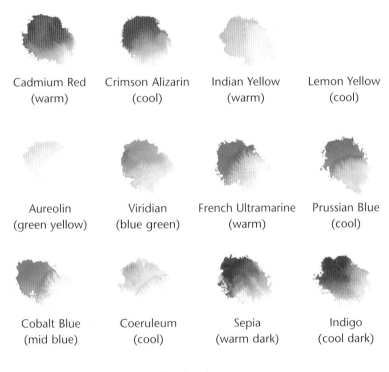

Cadmium Red (warm)

Crimson Alizarin (cool)

Indian Yellow (warm)

Lemon Yellow (cool)

Aureolin (green yellow)

Viridian (blue green)

French Ultramarine (warm)

Prussian Blue (cool)

Cobalt Blue (mid blue)

Coeruleum (cool)

Sepia (warm dark)

Indigo (cool dark)

Earth colours:

Yellow Ochre

Burnt Sienna

Burnt Umber

Choosing your colours

I cannot think of a watercolour pigment that is not vibrant before use. When mixed with water, colours that look dead in the pan come alive. Every artist will suggest a different range of colours. One way to choose your selection is to find an artist's work you admire and copy their list of colours. A useful range is suggested here. If you buy a ready-made palette the choice of colours is usually made for you, but you can fill empty palettes with pans or select your own tubes. My only reservation with a ready-made palette of pans is that beginners are tempted to dip into all the colours for each painting instead of limiting themselves to a few well-chosen pigments. Whatever you do I suggest you start with a maximum choice of 15 colours, but try to use no more than seven or eight at a time for each painting, and sometimes as few as three.

A tube of white gouache paint is an interesting addition, allowing you to create opaque colour, hazy tints and the restoration of small areas of white.

◄ Many papers in sheet form are available in sketchblocks as well. These pads are stuck down at the sides to prevent buckling. There are dozens of irresistible sketchbooks on the market. Choose a size that you will find convenient to carry around. Spiral-bound sketchbooks are easily available and pleasant to use, and hardback sketchbooks are great for memories.

Paper

Watercolour papers are available in different textures and weights. The most forgiving papers are medium-textured, Not surface with a weight of 300 gsm (140 lb) and upwards. However, highly textured, Rough paper will add character and intrigue to a painting, and smooth-surfaced HP paper will create wonderful backruns and watercolour effects. Why not experiment with each?

There is no set size for a painting, so just choose the dimensions you feel able to cope with. If you work large you will need to stick the paper firmly down to a board on all sides to prevent it buckling or otherwise use heavier paper.

Water, pencils and erasers

Small transparent glass or plastic pots make the best water containers. Empty film cassettes have watertight lids and are invaluable for outdoor sketching, and the cut-off bottoms of mineral-water bottles make good, light, disposable containers.

Carry plenty of clean water with you. Kitchen roll is the most practical rag paper.

For sketching under watercolour use a soft pencil, grades 2B to 6B, and a putty eraser, a gentle eraser that will not scuff the surface of the paper when you need to remove marks.

Extra materials

You can paint watercolours flat or tilted and, unless they are very wet, they can also be painted on an upright surface. You can see a painting better when it is on an easel, but it

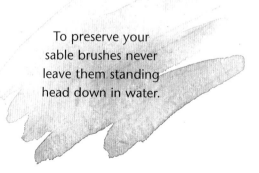

To preserve your sable brushes never leave them standing head down in water.

is easier to control the flow of paint when it is laid down. Ideally you want to be able to lift up and lay down a painting easily throughout the painting process. Any rigid board can be used for a drawing board: a piece of hardboard or plywood is fine.

A selection of different materials such as a natural sponge, masking fluid, a wax candle and salt crystals is useful for textured effects.

◄ There is no limit to the materials you can employ to make vibrant marks in watercolour. Here are some used in 'Textures and Surfaces' for creating a variety of different effects.

▼ **The Falls**
56 x 76 cm (22 x 30 in) The foreground spray is kept white with flicked masking fluid and the texture of the rock enhanced with the use of salt crystals.

How To Use Watercolour

The radiance and spontaneity of watercolour paint are two of its most attractive qualities. To make the most of these you will need to know how to mix and lay your colours. Mastery of technique will not guarantee vibrant paintings, but it will give your watercolours a chance to show you what they can do and you a chance to express yourself more succinctly.

Just add water

To release the wonderful pigments in watercolour paint you must dilute them with water. Not only do they become lighter in colour the more water you use, but they also often look very different in colour from their solid form. How much water to use is only gained by practice. Beginners often make their colours too wishy-washy or use them too thick, so that either a general dullness prevails or the painting is garish.

To load your brush with water for mixing, dip the whole body of the brush into clean water and as you lift it out roll it against the edge of the water jar to shape the point and remove some of the water.

If you want drier or more intense colour dab the water off the brush on a piece of kitchen paper before you touch the palette, turning the brush sideways on the paper in a fashion that keeps its tip pointed.

Translucence

Watercolour is a transparent medium that gains its radiance from light bouncing back from the white paper through the layers of thin colour on top. Watercolour paintings are made up of successive tints of colour, but if you paint too many layers on top of each other you will reduce or lose that transparency. Examine vibrant watercolours and you will find a minimum of overpainting. Make each layer count; it must be there for a reason. One or two rich washes will preserve radiance, whereas lots of layers will tend to dull a colour down.

◀ To mix a pale colour place the brush on to the pan of pigment and rub it with the tip of the brush only, to release the colour. Place this on the palette to check its strength and gather more from the pan until you have enough for the passage of painting involved.

◀ For larger, richer pools of colour twist the body of the brush in the pan, lifting the colour into the hairs of the brush. Lay this on the palette and keep adding from the pan until you have enough.

◀ The colours from tubes yield up their pigment far more readily than pans as they are already semi-liquid. Squeeze a little paint on to the palette. Take a little pigment, add water, then add a little more pigment until you reach the colour you desire.

▲ Each brush stroke is laid down quickly in a mark that describes the shapes within the flower.

Brush strokes

The initial brush strokes over virgin paper carry a vitality that overpainting may obscure. Paint with boldness, laying down your colours in shapes that are meaningful rather than indiscriminate. The joy of watercolour painting is that you build up an image with areas of colour rather than outlines. The brush stroke itself has a power of description, so harness that characteristic to create evocative paintings.

Take time to mix the right strength of colour before you add the brush stroke to your painting. Testing colours on the painting and adding layers and layers of hopeful washes to strengthen a colour is a

▶ The body of the tomato is just one broad circular-shaped brush stroke of Cadmium Red. While still wet more red is touched into the left-hand side, immediately suggesting three-dimensional form.

▲ To suggest a treeline different greens and browns are dabbed into the base of the wet sky wash and allowed to spread.

▲ The silhouette of the tree is created with the tip of a fully loaded round brush in one continual wash without seams.

▲ A blue wash is painted in shapes equivalent to the shadows on the boy. Burnt Sienna is then laid in brush strokes that colour the skin and dark areas of clothes.

◀ The dry-brush strokes on the bark follow the shape of the tree to suggest its form.

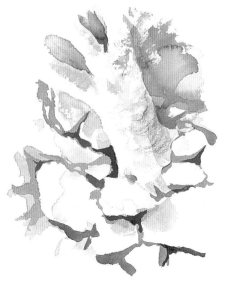

recipe for disaster. The lovely broken edge of a first wash as it caresses the tooth of the paper will be lost underneath successive brush strokes and the life of the painting will be gone.

Most said with minimum means

Imagine you are allowed only 50 brush strokes per painting. You would take care to get each one right. You would make sure each time you laid your brush down that it carried the desired colour to the chosen place and made the required shape – no dithering with meaningless brush marks or insipid layers of colour. You would spend more time mixing in the palette and more time looking at the subject. In a successful watercolour more time is spent off the paper than on it. A painting's success is no less deserved because it is arrived at quickly.

Painting techniques

There are two main techniques to apply watercolour to paper, and in general you will use a combination of the two: wet-in-wet and wet-on-dry.

Wet-in-wet

The technique of allowing one colour to run into another while it is still wet is called wet-in-wet. As the colours merge they create gentle grading and soft evocative effects. If lots of water and pigment are used dynamic explosions of colour occur as backruns push pigment into unpredictable patterns.

Atmospheric washes

You can dampen the whole, or parts, of the paper with clear water and then run your colour into this to create soft atmospheric washes – for hazy skies, for instance. Mix a good quantity of colour, use a large brush and lay the colour across the dampened page in successive slightly overlapping washes. If you want the wash to be paler at the bottom gradually dilute the mix as you go. Tilt the

▲ To paint wet-in-wet prepare the colours in sufficient quantities first. Touching in the second colour at the right moment takes practice. If the first colour is too wet the second will run quickly into it, but the longer you wait the more slowly it spreads.

▶ **Walking the Dog**
28 x 36 cm (11 x 14 in)
A variegated wash occurs if you lay several colours onto the wetted paper. This thundery sky results from Yellow Ochre, Burnt Sienna, Sepia, Prussian Blue and Indigo intermingling on the wet paper.

paper to encourage an even flow, and do not fiddle with perceived imperfections in the wash as it is drying.

Wet-on-dry

Radiant, lively watercolours are created with this method. The watercolour is painted on to the dry paper and allowed to dry completely before successive layers of colour are laid on top. The overlapping washes are crisp edged and glowing, especially if some of the previous colour is left untouched by the colour laid next. Uneven pooling of the colour as it dries can add to its charm, so avoid the temptation to 'perfect' the wash. Leave it to dry unmolested.

Using both techniques

You can combine both techniques in any watercolour painting. You can also lay a wet-in-wet wash over a dried wash by wetting it slightly with clear water. Brush the second colour on so that it blends into the wet area over the first colour. Always wet the paper well beyond the area you wish the paint to

spread, or you will end up with a hard edge where the paint meets the edge of the water. Make sure the wash underneath is completely dry before you rewet it or you will disturb it and ruin its quality.

▲ Thin veils of colour laid wet-on-dry overlap each other to build up the forms, colours and shapes in this cheerful little sketch of a fruit bowl.

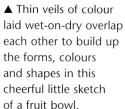

◄ Grantchester Meadows
28 x 36 cm (11 x 14 in)
To create soft foliage the paper is damped with clear water over the dried underwash of pale geen. Darker green is brushed on wet-in-wet and spreads softly into the damped area. Wet-on-dry brush strokes create contrasting crisp marks.

15

► Fine hairy lines can be created by actually splaying the hairs of the brush apart after loading with paint. To create the grasses I dragged a splayed round brush upward across the paper to release the paint. For the birch bark I used a flat brush and took the splayed stroke around the trees to help shape the trunks.

Dry-brush

The ragged edge of the dry-brush stroke is a marvellous counterfoil to the soft edges of wet-in-wet colour. To make dry-brush marks tap off all excess moisture from your brush on the rag and mix your paint with very little water. On a rough paper the brush stroke will create a delightful and often dramatic broken edge as it scumbles over the tooth of the paper.

Reserving white paper

Despite the fact that watercolour paper is seldom bright white, the highlights and lightest lights you can obtain in watercolour are created by leaving the white paper unpainted.

The freshest method of reserving the white paper is simply to avoid painting over it by careful observation or around a drawn guideline. The slightly irregular shapes left between passages of paint are another of the most appealing characteristics of watercolour. Take note of the lightest parts of your painting, and leave them as white paper from the start and throughout the painting. If later on you wish to tint them nothing is lost.

► Kensington Gardens
13 x 18 cm (5 x 7 in)
Looking into the light creates haloes around lit objects backed by a dark background. What better way to create this light in a painting than by leaving areas of white paper between the highlit figures and the background of foliage?

wet wash, or for an immediate correction. Once the wash is dry it is still possible to lift off the colour to some or almost all the extent by rubbing the required area gently with a damp brush or sponge and dabbing off the loosened pigment.

White paint

White gouache can be used for retrieving small highlights, and you might find it easier on occasion than trying to paint round tiny areas or lines of white paper. Colour can also be added to the gouache to create a tinted light if you wish.

A thin wash of white will make a colour look less vivid. Paint a dilute wash across the colour like a veil and then leave it to dry without touching it.

▲ Masking fluid was used to protect the blades of corn from the variegated wash. The unmasked shapes are apt to look blobby unless they are quite carefully painted with attention to their shape. After the masking is removed the stalks are touched in with pale Yellow Ochre.

Masking fluid is an oft-used timesaver for protecting the white paper during the painting. It is a latex fluid, resistant to water. Paint it on at the start over details you wish to keep white, and rub it off when the paint is dry to reveal untouched white paper.

Lifting out

While watercolour is wet it is possible to dab it off almost without stain. You can use this technique for retrieving highlights from a

▶ The bright orange wash is painted on to wet paper and the sun and its reflection are lifted off immediately with a piece of kitchen roll. The colour is then dragged across the path of the sun from either side to create gentle ripples.

▲ A size 4 brush with a fine tip and neat moist white gouache enables you to paint the detail of railings over a dark background.

Confident Colour

Colour has a predominant part to play in creating vibrant watercolours. Not only do individual colours affect other colours, but particular colours provoke different reactions in the viewer. The groupings of similar or opposite colours can also evoke a specific mood or atmosphere in a painting. Exploiting the properties of colour will help you create striking pictures.

Colour theory certainly helps in the understanding of how to use colour, but, as with everything in painting, it is practice that counts. I find it better to experiment in actual paintings than with colour swatches.

◀ **Venetian Corners**
76 x 56 cm (30 x 22 in)
This watercolour is full of colour, and yet the palette consists of just six colours, a warm and cool version of the three primaries: Cadmium Red and Crimson Alizarin, Yellow Ochre and Aureolin, Cobalt Blue and Prussian Blue.

Basic colours

In painting red, yellow and blue are called primary colours because all other colours can be made from mixing two or three of them together. Secondary colours are so called because they are the colours we obtain from mixing just two of the primaries together. Thus red and yellow make orange, blue and yellow make green, and red and blue make purple.

Interaction of colour

No colour is absolute. Colours change under different lights and against different hues and tones. Colours juxtaposed can enhance or detract from each other. A red next to a green or turquoise will vibrate with excitement. Put a blue next to an orange and both colours will look brighter. Mauve and yellow, when placed adjacent, will make the other colour appear stronger.

What is the reason for this interaction? Each of the pairs of colours mentioned includes a primary and a secondary colour, which, if both were mixed together, would then include all three primary colours. These paired combinations are called opposite colours because each is as different from the other as a colour can be. They are also called complementary colours because together they comprise the three primaries. The artist can make use of these properties to help colours stand out or to mute colours that are too bright.

When you mix the three primaries together you can make any number of browns, greys, and ultimately blacks. It follows, therefore, that if two opposite colours are mixed together they will also make those greys, browns and blacks.

▼ **Crossing the Kalahari**
43 x 76 cm (17 x 30 in)
The contrasting complementary colours of blue and orange are used to dynamic effect in this painting of gemsbok crossing the harsh stark dunes of the Kalahari desert.

Warm and cool colours

Another vital ingredient for the artist to understand is the 'temperature' of colours.

If you wish to evoke a cool atmosphere use more blue colours in your painting. If you want to create warmth and excitement you must play with reds and oranges.

This warmth or coolness is relative. Each colour that is not a pure primary leans towards another; thus Crimson Alizarin is a red, but it is a purple-red and veers toward blue. It is, therefore, a cool red even though it is a warm colour in relation to blue. The selection of colours suggested in 'Materials and Equipment' included a warm and a cool version of each colour.

By mixing colours of like temperature you can create colours that are more vivid than if you mix a warm and a cool colour together. To make bright colours, therefore, mix two together that have the same temperature; for example, Cadmium Red and Cadmium Yellow. For duller colours mix two of different temperatures; for example, French Ultramarine and Yellow Ochre.

Seeing colour

When you look at an object or a landscape, never presume that you already know the colour. Nothing remains the same as the light upon it changes. A white wall may glow rose with the reflected light from terracotta tiles, or turn blue as it is cast in shadow.

Watercolour lends itself to the exaggeration of reflected colour. Its gentle tints and overlaying washes can warm up or cool down any passage of colour at a stroke. As you look more closely you will notice colours that you did not expect to be there. That alone is an exciting discovery, and then to be able to emulate those colours with paint is an inspiration in itself.

If you remember that you are playing with tints rather than opaque colour, then

▲ **Umbrella against the Sun**
15 x 20 cm (6 x 8 in)
▶ **In the Stillness**
25 x 36 cm (10 x 14 in)
By comparing these two paintings of African trees you can see the warmth that red confers on a painting and the cool calm effect brought by blue.

◀ The lemon, brightly lit, reflects some of its own colour on to the cloth.

▶ Yellow Ochre laid over the bodies of the mushrooms and shadow modifies the blue underwash, making it into an interesting warm grey.

you can be braver in your use of colour. All colours mixed together make brown or grey. With watercolour you are effectively 'mixing' by overlaying coloured layers. Therefore, although you may be painting with a bright colour it will be modified by the colour underneath or on top. As a painter you are not obliged to copy the colours of the material world, but can approximate to or even change colours as you wish.

Be brave

Do not be afraid of colour. Timidity never made successful paintings. You can always dull down a painting later on, but if you lose vibrancy at the start it is hard to retrieve it. No colour is wrong in itself; it is only in relation to others that it might not look right. Only when it is down on the paper does instinct tell you it needs perhaps to be more blue, or less bright. The beauty of watercolour is that then you can alter it, overlaying it with a tint of blue or a thin wash of its complementary to dull it down.

Vibrant watercolour paintings are not made up of wishy-washy colours. Think before you paint. Be positive in your choice of colour, definite in your mixes and bold in your application.

◀ **Boats in Burano**
38 x 56 cm (15 x 22 in)
Boats are often brightly painted. They are a great subject for practising brave colour. Here the hulls and reflections merge together wet-in-wet.

Seizing the Moment

By now you will be itching to make paintings. No doubt you have seen something that sets the visual juices flowing, but you are not feeling brave enough to try a finished picture.

This is where a sketchbook can come to the rescue. It starts off as being a handy way to record things you see and to make instant paintings without regard to composition or finish. It often ends up containing the most vibrant examples of an artist's work, because it is not trying to be anything else. Choose a sketchbook that fits into your life. A size that pops into the pocket, handbag, or briefcase, or that wedges behind your belt, is ideal.

A practical sketchbook

Hardback sketchbooks tend to have a lasting appeal because once filled they can sit happily on a bookshelf for easy retrieval. You can date them on the spine and build up a visual diary of your life. Softback sketchbooks are usually slimmer, with the

▼ Go out with a sketchbook and make quick paintings of scenes and incidents that appeal. Painting is a 'doing' word – you do not improve by just thinking about it!

a gaggle of gulls Aldeburgh.

advantage that you can easily remove leaves of paper, either to frame up successful sketches, or to give as gifts.

Whatever you choose, use it. Make written as well as visual notes while waiting for people, on the bus, in the café. Care not what the finished result looks like. Examine with the eyes, interpret with the brush.

Exercising the eye

Vibrant watercolours come from inside just as much as from outside. How you react to what you see is crucial to the success of your painting. If you cannot see the shadow from a pot, for instance, as integral to that pot you will paint it separately and the painting will look disjointed. Use your sketchbook to stretch your vision. Notice how different units combine together. Look at the shapes of the spaces between objects, rather than the things themselves. All this can be practised in the sketchbook on a small and unembarassing scale.

Collecting reference

Sometimes you will be able to use your sketches to help make larger paintings. In that case you may need to make colour notes on the sketches themselves. There are no rules, everything is permissible.

Using the camera as a sketchbook can also be helpful for freezing quick movements and drawing specific shapes. Painting from photographs is not a very good way to learn, because the camera cannot see in the same way that you do. It treats everything as equally important whereas you home in on something particular. However, once you are confident at painting from life, you will probably find the photograph a useful reference tool.

Above all, using a sketchbook keeps you visually well tuned. If you are not in a position to paint regularly it will at least maintain the momentum.

▶ Cats move quickly, so a size 3 brush loaded with black ink and a small pot of water ready to dilute it are all you need to explore their shapes.

◀ Even a simple sketch of a child's toy in a hotel room carries so much weight in years to come. When I drew this I was just passing time, but now my son is older the sketch actually marks the passing time.

The Heart of the Subject

For a painting to be vibrant the subject need not be profound. The most interesting paintings often have very humble subject matter. Think of Van Gogh's chair, Mona Lisa's smile, or Chardin's apples – they are all vibrant paintings of simple subjects. These paintings catch our imagination because they convey the essence of the subject, though it may be just a fleeting moment.

Keep it simple

While you are learning to paint keep the subject of your paintings simple and direct. If you are painting a landscape, then place yourself in it. Look around. Ask yourself what interests you? It could be the shape of the tree trunk or the long shadows in stripes on the grass. It may be the bleaching effect of the sun as it strips colour from the edges it strikes. In a still life it might be the tiny gap between the handle of a sugar bowl and a jug, or the light bouncing out of a rim.

The subject in question

Some subjects, such as beautiful scenery or exciting colours, have a more universal appeal than others. Beginners to painting are often drawn towards these subjects as they reap such pleasure from them in 'real life' and long to be able to represent them on paper. However, these are often quite challenging compositions. So how do you tackle them?

First you need to decide what the actual subject of your painting is. Simply ask yourself, 'What do I like best about this scene?', 'What has attracted me?'. It might be the light, the atmosphere, the small houses against the sky, a particular tree or one colour found among others in a bunch of

▶ **The Breeze**
30 x 20 cm (11 x 8 in)
In the house opposite my studio was a little window with a net curtain. One day the lower sash window was lifted and a gentle breeze caught the net. Suddenly I wanted to paint that window, but the subject was not the window itself; it was the effect of the breeze upon it.

flowers. Once you have chosen your subject the scene becomes the vehicle for drawing attention to this interest. The artist, you, will bring to the viewers' attention something they might not have noticed before, or something you have seen or felt but never crystallized in words.

The main attraction

Whatever the subject is, jot it down beside the painting to remind yourself as you go along. Start your painting or sketch with the main interest, maybe just faintly mapped in, but noted from the outset. As you build up your painting ask yourself continuously is this still the main event, have you focused on it, or have you given equal emphasis to other elements that now distract from it?

It may sound exaggerated to suggest all else surrenders to this subject, but it actually makes it much easier on the artist. If you are painting the light falling on the window beside a vase of flowers, there will come a point when you have painted that light reasonably successfully. Then you will hear a voice inside your head say, 'But more detail is needed in the flowers', or 'The line of the vase is not accurate'. Ask yourself if these things are interfering with the painting of the light. If not, they are best left alone and the painting is finished.

Overworking a painting is a problem that all artists face. Knowing when to stop is much easier if you set your goal and recognize when you have reached it.

▶ **Lazy Morning**
56 x 41 cm (22 x 16 in)
The subject of this painting is not the sofa, the geraniums or the newspaper, but the light streaming through the window – that glorious summer light that steals the colour from the surface on which it falls. The corner of the sunlit room is the vehicle chosen to express that light.

▶ **Sea Horses**
30 x 38 cm (12 x 15 in)
The attraction of this painting was not the horses, or the place, but a wonderful hazy atmosphere felt at dawn by the sea. To keep the sense of mood intact I simplified the background mountains and the waves, and merely suggested details on the riders and their steeds.

◄ **The Shadow**
56 x 76 cm (22 x 30 in)
▼ **The Palm and its Shadow**
76 x 56 cm (30 x 22 in)
The dramatic shadow of the palm tree was my subject in these two pictures. In the painting on the left I emphasized just that. However, I became fascinated with the fronds of the palm tree itself, and as I could not fit them into my composition I started again with the paper turned vertically. Changing one's mind is the artist's prerogative!

Changing your mind

A painting takes place over time, however short, and sometimes as you look and paint the main interest changes. You may start off excited by one particular element, but as you explore the subject visually something else takes on a greater interest. That is fine. You are in charge of the painting, and you can change your mind, but you must follow your thoughts through. A painting about everything is confusing. The viewer looks and thinks, 'Yes, attractive scene, but what is the painting about?' Unless the viewer can sense that you have an interest beyond the obvious physical subject of the painting they will probably be unmoved. Though they may be impressed by your talent or effort they will probably feel uninspired.

Your painting must stand alone from the subject when it is finished. You are free to emphasize or neglect whatever you think works best for the painting's success.

Subtlety and ambiguity

Sometimes your interest will be obvious; at other times less so. Subtlety and ambiguity are two of watercolour's most engaging assets. To suggest rather than state allows the viewer to participate. Watercolour's wet-on-dry veils and wet-in-wet blends encourage mystery. Loose brush marks can say so much. Use these attributes to encourage the viewer to become involved.

Integrity

The beauty of painting is that to different people one painting may mean different things. Here is the wonderful paradox of painting: if you are true to your own integrity, painting what you want the way you want, your painting will probably have more appeal than if you try to please other people instead of yourself.

▲ Sometimes you might try to tackle subjects that are less physical. This was the sketch for some canvas paintings about the intimacy between a mother and a child. I feel that this Sepia wash caught that tenderness with a few strokes of the brush.

◀ **Red Splash**
20 x 28 cm (8 x 11 in)
A simple subject is brought alive by the merging colours, brisk brush strokes and lack of definition. No item is painted precisely but we know exactly what is represented.

Creative Composition

Paintings can be vibrant and lively simply because the composition is successful. Composition is the design of the painting upon the paper. A little forethought and planning can make a painting more effective, so, before you even begin, decide if the actual piece of paper you are going to use is the right shape and the right size for the picture you want to make.

Having chosen your surface, next plan the layout of the image on the paper.

Viewfinder

Using a viewfinder really helps in planning a painting. Two L-shaped pieces of card placed together to make a variable rectangle are ideal. Hold these out in front of you to form a rectangular window and view your chosen subject through this. Remind yourself of the real subject, the reason for your interest in this particular scene or group of objects. Move the viewfinder around, and back and forth, until you feel a satisfactory balance in the arrangement bounded by the edges of the card. If the view does not readily make a satisfactory composition be prepared to move objects in your actual painting. Do not become such a slave to the view that your painting suffers. The painting comes first.

Three into two does go

A representational painting is a two-dimensional image of a three-dimensional subject. In planning your composition,

◄ To experiment with composition I rearranged this group of objects several times. One advantage of painting the same subject in different arrangements is that it prevents you overworking any one painting, but gives you a chance to enjoy the subject over a longer period of time.

▶ San Giorgio from Schiavoni
41 x 56 cm (16 x 22 in)
The focal point of this painting is the church in the distance. The lines of the gondolas lead the eye towards this, but not so blatantly that the composition becomes too obvious.

therefore, you need only look at the two-dimensional arrangement of the shapes, colours, lines and spaces of the view in front of you. The very fact that you desire to paint means you are probably already visually aware of naturally good compositions as they occur around you. Trust your judgement as to when you think the image looks interesting or balanced.

Focal point

Most paintings benefit from a main focal point of interest in order to draw the viewer's attention. It could be a specific item or a general incident, and is usually the subject of the painting. As you look through the viewfinder move the main interest of your painting to either side of the centre line and up and down. In general a feature of interest looks more dynamic away from the centre. Likewise in a landscape the horizon is better placed either above or below the horizontal centre-line of the painting. If it helps, look at paintings you admire and transfer their compositions to your own subject matter.

Sketching your composition

Remember you are only concerned at this stage with a two-dimensional surface. Imagine your viewfinder has a glass pane. If you could trace the view beyond it on to the glass that would be a similar design to the drawing you want on the paper.

Point your finger into the viewfinder at the focal point. Find the equivalent position on your paper and make a dot. Start your drawing from there.

You do not need a highly detailed drawing for most watercolour painting. The sketch should be a guide for the brush simply to tell it where it can and cannot go. Sketch loosely so that you can change your mind with little or no erasure. View your sketch at a short distance to make sure you are happy with the design before you go any further.

▶ Conservatory
76 x 56 cm (30 x 22 in)
The subject of this painting is the diffuse light in a glass room rather than any particular items in the conservatory. If your subject is general rather than specific you can still use the composition to lead the eye into the painting.

▶ It can be hard for beginners to accept how small a figure in the distance will be beside a figure in the foreground.

▶ **In the Shadow of Nelson's Column**
28 x 20 cm (11 x 8 in)
By holding a pencil to measure the size of the foreground pigeons and then comparing it with the size of the pigeons in the background the relative proportions are easily found.

Relative scale

Once you have arranged your composition loosely on the paper you can be more specific with the shapes and sizes of the items you portray. Keep in mind the chief inspiration for your painting and still use this as your starting point as you add detail and correct or enhance the drawing. By cross-referring with imaginary horizontal and vertical lines from one object to another you can find and plot the position of everything in relation to the main feature.

Hold your pencil out in front of you and measure the close and distant items in relation to the length of the pencil. By comparing their sizes you will see the difference in scale clearly. The age-old joke of the artist squinting with one eye at his outstretched thumb is none other than this method of measuring!

By cross-reference you will automatically achieve the right scale for various items.

The shapes in between

The shapes between items are as vital to the flat two-dimensional world of the paper as the size and shape of objects themselves. Some artists term these 'negative' shapes, but

▲ Find the correct curve of the handles on a cup and jug by drawing the shape of the gaps between the body and the handle of each item.

▶ It is much easier to draw the limbs of a figure if you first assess the angles and shape between those limbs. The pose will then quickly fall into place.

▲ Try to see in shape rather than line. This unfinished sketch defines the shapes of the girls on the bench by painting the spaces between them and around them.

they are just as important as the shapes inside objects and seeing them clearly will make drawing much easier. When someone stands with their elbow bent and their hand on their waist, look at the shape of the space made between the arm and the body. In the landscape look for the shapes between buildings and under trees.

To practise this, set yourself the task of defining a whole composition by drawing only the shapes in between items and not the actual items themselves.

Check the overall shapes of objects, figures, fields etc. by using the outstretched pencil method to compare the height of an object with its width. Adjust your drawing to compensate for errors of judgement.

Linking shapes

Grouped subjects look more coherent if they are bound together by invisible lines. We do not see things separately, but as parts of a whole. Use the same vision in your painting.

Viewing your painting in a mirror enables you to see errors of drawing more easily.

▲ **Rush Hour**
13 x 18 cm (5 x 7 in)
Instead of seeing objects as separate entities attach them together by merging colours, either by working wet-in-wet or overlaying linking washes. Subjects and their shadows often dissolve one into another. Highlights, too, will blur the lines of separation.

Suggesting Form and Space

Creating the illusion of the third dimension on a two-dimensional plane is one of the most exciting aspects of painting. Even after years of painting, I still find it utterly magical that I can start with a blank sheet of paper and end up with something that has its own life.

Making objects look three-dimensional is easier than you think. As we are used to seeing things in the round in our physical world, it takes very little to suggest that something in your painting has three-dimensional form. From experience the viewer already presumes it has.

There are two main ways of creating form. One is by outline and shape, the other is through the use of tone.

The outline

How do you draw a round object on a flat piece of paper? Look again through your viewfinder, and imagine it as a pane of glass. Trace the lines describing the surfaces of objects turning away from you and see how they tilt up or down on the flat picture plane. Use your pencil to find their angles, holding it parallel to the viewfinder. These angles are governed by the laws of perspective, but you need not study perspective to be able to assess the angle of tilt correctly. The information is all in front of you; you only have to copy exactly what you see.

You will notice that at your eye-level the lines are all straight, but as they fall below your eye-level they tilt up towards it, and as they rise above your eye-level they tilt down towards it. By accurate observation and cross-referencing to other items you can find how steeply or gently the lines tilt. Copy these angles as closely as possible on to the flat paper and you will see the forms taking shape in perspective and looking three-dimensional. The more you observe and practise the easier this becomes.

Variation of tone

With your drawing you may have suggested roundness or bulk with the curve or angle of the line, but you have at your disposal an even more persuasive tool – tone. Tone is the lightness or darkness of an object.

Tone is described by a scale ranging from white through greys to black. Thus a dark tone would be a dark grey, and a light tone a pale grey. When colour is added to tone the

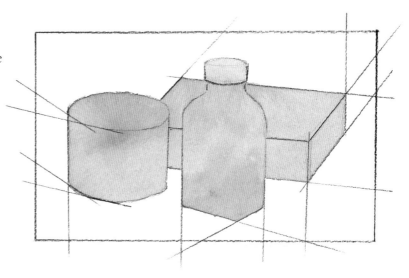

▲ Outline: By copying the tilt of the lines on the flat picture plane, outlines can be built up and three-dimensional form is suggested.

▼ Tone: The outline drawing of these items gives no clue that they are solid forms, but the variation of tone across the surfaces persuades us that the objects are not flat.

▲ Outline and Tone: If we put together a drawing outline that suggests form and paint a variation of tone that suggests form we are convinced that these forms are three-dimensional.

same scale of lightness and darkness occurs within the range of the colour. Even though a ball might be the colour red, around its circumference several different tones of red will be at play. Using this differentiation of tone from the local colour (the perceived colour of the object) enables the artist to suggest its form.

Light source

When an object is lit from one source, such as the sun or a lamp, light falls directly on one surface, but leaves the others in varying

degrees of shadow. The side upon which no light falls may be very dark. If there is a lot of ambient light around then these unlit sides will receive a measure of reflected light from all around, but will still be darker than the side facing the light.

When you are planning your composition, bear in mind the source of light. A view with the light source directly in front will not have such an interesting variation of tone as if the light source comes from the side, or slightly behind. Morning and evening will also give you more interesting lights and shadows than a subject that is painted under a noonday sun.

▼ Rock Painting
53 x 74 cm (21 x 29 in)
The strong light source from above lights the top of the rocks, while the sides are given a colourful mid tone. The darkest tones are used in the crevices under the rocks. Just three tones convince us easily of the solidity of these rocks while the colours create the soft ethereal nature of the place.

▶ Imagine three similar-sized trees, each further away, on a road leading to the horizon. If you draw a line across the top and bottom those lines will meet at the horizon. The diminishing size tells us that the trees are receding in space.

Space and distance

Creating the illusion of space in a painting is also about perspective. The horizon is always at eye-level, and all lines leading away from the eye eventually meet at the horizon. Similar-sized objects as they recede look smaller in relation to each other. (See 'Relative scale' in 'Creative Composition'.)

Thus objects and figures in the foreground will appear larger than their equivalents in the background. The viewer has no trouble believing this because they have seen it in real life. You need, therefore, only put the suggestion into their mind and use this fact to enhance the perception of space in your paintings. The greater the difference in size the more distance suggested.

▼ Fields at Harvest
20 x 28 cm (8 x 11 in)
The relative size of the foreground trees to the ones in the middle distance and those at the horizon convinces the viewer that this is a large open space.

◄ The three trees are all the same size and on the same picture plane, but by lightening the tone from left to right we suggest that the two lighter ones are receding. Likewise, the hills appear to recede into the distance as the tones become paler. Overlapping objects enhances this illusion.

Using tone and colour

We have already seen how powerfully tone describes form, but you can also use tone to suggest distance. Strong dark colours seem to jump forward, while pale colours recede. Therefore, if you paint the far distance lighter than the foreground you will persuade the viewer that space exists within your painting, creating the illusion of depth on the flat paper. Practise comparing the colour of distant hills, mountains or buildings when out in the landscape. They may seem dark in relation to the sky, but if you half close your eyes and match them against something dark in the foreground, you will see how much darker that nearer item will be.

Colour can also help you create space. Reds assert themselves, whereas blues recede. However, since no colour exists without tone (its lightness or darkness) ultimately tone is the more powerful painting tool.

Carry a piece of black card in your pocket and use it to compare the darks and mid tones of the subject you are painting.

◄ The Long White Beach
28 x 36 cm (11 x 14 in)
All the artist's tools of illusion are brought into play to suggest the length of this very long beach on the flat surface of paper that is no larger than a window pane. The dramatically diminishing size of the rocks suggests great distance, the paler background tones of the hills recede and the warm foreground colours of the rocks jump forward. Perspective, tone and colour – what a trio!

The Power of Contrast

Now that you have used tone to suggest three-dimensional form and the illusion of depth you will realize how important it is in the structure of a painting. The greater the contrast of tone within an image the more vibrant and dramatic the final visual effect.

A strong directional light source causes strong tonal contrasts. Bright light through a door throws the rest of the room into shadow. A form lit from behind becomes a silhouetted shape of light against dark. This strong contrast of light and dark transferred to your watercolour makes an arresting painting. A sense of drama is intrinsic in the dark and lightness portrayed.

▲ **Chelsea Arts Club**
18 x 13 cm (7 x 5 in)
An ordinary subject of a jacket draped over the back of a chair is transformed into a vibrant little painting by the dramatic shaft of light cast across the restaurant floor.

Mixing dark colours

To create lively dark areas in your painting, forget ready-made colours such as Black or Payne's Grey. Instead make those dark tones out of two opposite colours, such as blues and browns, or reds and greens. The effects will be rich, dark, slightly variable washes that are full of mystery.

The combinations are endless, and the colours delicious. Mix lots of pigment with enough water to make a creamy mixture. But take care that it is not too thick or you may find that an unwanted sheen appears on the dried surface of the wash.

Remember that very wet watercolour dries lighter than it appears when wet. So, if you think your wash is going to dry too light and it is still wet, plunge more pigment into the wash wet-in-wet.

These darks can be built up in layers, but too many layers will deaden the colour, so try to reach the colour you desire with your first or second wash.

◄ Here are some suggested combinations to make vibrant darks.
Top row: French Ultramarine and Burnt Sienna, French Ultramarine and Burnt Umber, French Ultramarine and Sepia, French Ultramarine and Raw Umber.
Middle row: Prussian Blue and Burnt Sienna, Prussian Blue and Burnt Umber, Prussian Blue and Sepia, Prussian Blue and Raw Umber.
Bottom row: Indigo and Sepia, Crimson Alizarin and Indigo, Crimson Alizarin and Viridian.

The highlights

It is the difference between the light and dark that counts in a painting using tonal contrast, so pay close attention to the lightest areas. The white paper will always represent your lightest highlights. Demarcate those areas you want to remain white in your preliminary sketch and be careful not to paint over them by mistake.

To make the brightest highlights stand out other light areas can be tinted with thin transparent washes to lessen their brightness.

Shadows

Shadows, like the dark areas in a painting, also benefit from being coloured rather than grey. At sunset the blue or mauve cast to a shadow is very obvious, but even during the day shadows are tinted with colour. It behoves the artist to seek out and emphasize these colours, even if at first you do not believe you see them. Watercolour has the advantage of being transparent, enabling you to lay tints of colour over other colours and thus create coloured shadows that can, if necessary, be modified by other colours on top or that shine through from underneath. Remember that overlaying three primary colours will turn them to greys and browns.

▲ **Beachcombing**
23 x 15 cm (9 x 6 in)
I love to paint silhouettes against the setting sun. I used masking fluid to hold back the highlights of the sparkles on the water from the all-over Yellow Ochre and Indigo wash.

◄ **Singing the Blues**
76 x 56 cm (30 x 22 in)
The warmth of French Ultramarine is used to paint the shadows of the flowers and pillow. Contrasted with the stronger French Ultramarine of the cornflowers and the bright yellow chrysanthemums there is no need to modify the blue towards a grey; it already settles back to become a believable shadow.

Colour contrast

Contrast is not just about tone. By contrasting opposite or complementary colours you can also achieve dynamic effects. For a vibrant, colourful watercolour, contrast red with green, purple with yellow or orange with blue.

These contrasts need not be blatant; remember that subtlety and suggestion are very persuasive. An orange flower set in green foliage that veers to blue will be more striking, and look more orange, than if the foliage green veers to yellow. Use the temperature of colours to create contrast too. Warm reds placed against cool blues will look hotter than cool reds against warm blues. A painting of a blue sky against a warm Yellow Ochre beach will look brighter than if you paint the beach with a cold Lemon Yellow.

Vibrant greys

For mid greys, mix the two-colour combinations suggested on page 36, and dilute with more water. Sometimes you will obtain a wonderful granulating effect as the two colours separate grain from grain on the surface of the paper. This adds texture to the

▼ Paradise Found
56 x 76 cm (22 x 30 in)
Africa is hot – the hippos are returning to water. I have used the dramatic contrast of yellow and purple to evoke the excitement I felt at this scene.

Marsh Harriers hunting over Lac Fortuna Danube Delta 24.9.96

▲ **Danube Delta**
20 x 25 cm (8 x 10 in)
This vast expanse of water and marsh fascinated me. By lowering my eyeline I could break up the soft wet-in-wet wash with angular grasses to bring the sketch to life.

shadow. French Ultramarine and Burnt Sienna will often do this, as will Coeruleum or Manganese Blue and Yellow Ochre, but it does not always happen!

Greys made from two colours will have more character than ready-made greys. You can easily veer them towards the colour you perceive the grey to be – for example, a blue-grey or a green-grey – by adding more of that particular colour in the mix.

Contrast of shape and line

Within a painting contrasts of every kind serve to enhance their opposite number. We have looked at contrast of tone and colour. What about contrast of shape and line?

A painting of soft undefined areas can lack interest, but if you introduce a contrasting angular shape the soft forms come alive. A landscape view of horizontal fields may well be attractive enough, but the vertical addition of a tree makes the composition sing.

These points may seem obvious when you see a naturally interesting view, but there will be times when you need to bring them to mind deliberately to make the composition lively. You may wish to paint a particular scene and you want it to be authentic to the physical nature of the place but the composition is boring. Try lowering your eyeline by sitting on the ground, so that foreground features rise up to cross the horizon and create a greater contrast of shape or line against the landscape. Look for ways that could make the painting more interesting. Trust your own judgement. If the composition interests you it will almost certainly interest someone else too.

Evoking Atmosphere and Mood

Vibrant watercolours can be strong and vital, exuding excitement, or they can be full of presence, atmosphere and calm. They can even reflect anxiety or foreboding.

How do we create a particular mood or atmosphere in the two-dimensional realm of the painting? It is possible to create atmosphere by using colours and techniques that affect the viewer's emotional response to the image. Not everyone reacts in the same way to the same stimuli, but there are colours that cheer and colours that quiet,

effects that are gentle on the eye and effects that excite or jar. These qualities alone will not make the painting work, however. They need to be supplemented by the artist's own emotional or spiritual input to truly inspire.

The effect of colour

In 'Confident Colour' we discovered that reds are generally active and blues more passive. Strong colours advance, while pale colours recede. These properties can be used

▼ **The Blue Lagoon**
30 x 38 cm (12 x 15 in)
The calmness pervading this painting is encouraged by the use of blue and the soft wet-in-wet blending of colours. I was in a peaceful mood when I painted it and felt a certain clarity in what I was doing. My mood has entered the painting.

St Tropez

Hazel Soan 94

by the artist to enhance the mood in the painting. If you want to create a cool, gentle atmosphere veer your overall colour scheme towards a harmony of greens and blues. Avoid too much strong tonal contrast without making your painting insipid. If you want drama and vitality use strong colours and contrast light and dark tones.

This is where you can employ the temperatures of colours to best effect. Keep asking yourself questions such as, 'Does this colour lean towards red or blue?', or 'Is it warm or cool?'. Just by varying the blue from a cool blue, such as Prussian Blue, to a warm blue, such as French Ultramarine, can change the whole mood of the painting.

Limit your palette

One of the problems for beginners is that they often use too many different colours within one painting and so dilute the properties of individual colours. Just because they are there in your palette does not mean that all the colours need to be used for each painting. Start by minimizing the colours used in any one painting. In a sky, for example, decide if you want to create a warm atmosphere or a cooler mood. If the former, choose a warm blue such as Cobalt or French Ultramarine; if cooler, use Prussian and continue the use of that blue throughout the painting.

▲ St Tropez
20 x 28 cm (8 x 11 in)
I wanted to create the 'tired' heat at the end of a hot Mediterranean day. To suggest warmth with a touch of the coming coolness of evening I chose Crimson Alizarin, a cool red. The only other colours I used were Yellow Ochre (warm) and French Ultramarine (warm). Using few colours guarantees the unity of the painting.

Coloured light

White paper is perfect for portraying the light of broad daylight, but a painting made at dawn or sunset, or in a firelit interior, needs an overall cast of colour to convince the viewer it is painted under a coloured light. To create this effect you can tint the whole paper at the outset with an overall pale wash of the colour you perceive the light to be, and then, when thoroughly dry, paint on top, leaving the lightest highlights as the tinted paper. This underwash of colour helps create the ambient light or atmosphere, and can be used to suggest a general warmth or coolness in a painting right from the start. You could also work on coloured watercolour paper.

Mix plenty of colour to a dilute wet consistency. Wet the paper first for a more even flow, then lay the colour with broad strokes so that each stroke merges wet-in-wet with the one before. Use spotlessly clean water to mix these transparent tints. Do not fiddle with the wash as it dries; any irritating imperfections will later disappear under the layers of painting on top.

Understatement and suggestion

One of the most intriguing qualities of watercolour is that more can often be said by suggestion than by detailed description.

▼ A cool light needs a cool colour. Here I have laid an overall wash of pale Prussian Blue and Coeruleum to create the atmosphere of wintry sunshine.

▼ A wash of Burnt Sienna, a few darker blobs across the middle and some upward streaks in the foreground: how little we need do with watercolour to suggest a landscape.

A few loose brush strokes at the horizon can make someone believe a whole mountain range exists. The more the viewer puts their own interpretation and imagination into your painting the more involved and interested they become.

To create mystery in a painting use the wet-in-wet technique. Let the colours dissolve together, so that shadows and the objects that cast them dissolve together with indefinable edges. Let features in the distance merge and let the clothes on a figure blend into the flesh. Do not try to exert too much control over all your washes. By limiting the flow of the watercolour you may be denying your painting the very life it craves. If a little paint runs into some unintended area do not automatically assume it will ruin your painting – it may well enhance it.

▼ **A Breath of Colour** 38 x 56 cm (15 x 22 in) Look closely at this painting of anemones and see how little actual detail has been painted. The edges of the flowers are often blurred with wet-in- wet washes and thin wet-on-dry veils of colour suggest overlapping petals. Everything is understated, yet perfectly understood, and a gentle atmosphere prevails.

Brush stroke and gesture

Using different papers and different brushes will help to create atmosphere and exciting effects, but more often than not it is the actual gesture of the brush stroke that contributes to the energy of the painting.

Paint, loosely applied, will create a livelier atmosphere than a painting made with stiff, nervous brush strokes. The life and character of brushwork is largely due to confidence.

The more you paint the fewer brush strokes you will lay, and the more meaningful each will become.

Sometimes what appears as abandon on the part of the artist is, in fact, quite carefully thought out. These brush strokes have only been laid when the right colour was mixed to the right consistency and aimed at the right place. The gesture may appear spontaneous, but it is actually loaded with thought and preparation.

▶ **Juarati**
56 x 43 cm (22 x 17 in)
In this painting the washes are allowed a measure of freedom. I worked with a large sable brush with a good point, sweeping the paint on in meaningful brush strokes. The rough paper adds the thrilling element of texture.

◄ **Evening Stroll**
18 x 25 cm (7 x 10 in)
There is an air of mystery to this evening stroll along the beach. The confidence of the dry-brush strokes contrasts well with the loose wet-in-wet washes and the figures and their reflections are put in boldly with a quick flick of the tip of the brush.

▼ If you choose subjects that you love you will see that genuine affection come out in the painting. Try making sketches of your family and friends doing things they enjoy.

Character

The spirit with which you paint will imbue the painting. If you are happy and relaxed the painting will have that joy and lightness of spirit. If you are frustrated and dissatisfied the painting will be lacklustre too. You do not need to be 'in the mood' to paint, however. You can start a painting feeling wholly separate from it and yet as you progress you will become completely involved. It is your commitment to the painting that counts. The more you put into a painting, not in terms of detail, but in observation, concentration, decision, animation and love, the more integrity your painting will have.

If you are painting indoors, listening to music while you paint can also affect and enhance the mood of your painting.

Freedom of Movement

The portrayal of movement within a painting can liven up any composition. Swift brush strokes and blurred edges suggest activity. If you are including people in a scene, painting their shapes as if they are in the process of moving looks far more interesting than static figures. Even if their shapes seem inaccurate you will be surprised how much you can get away with just by suggesting movement. The eye will complete the action.

Sketching moving subjects

Practise sketching and painting moving figures in a sketchbook. Then, when you need them for a finished painting, you can copy them on to the watercolour with more confidence. As you sketch with a brush or a pencil keep your eye on the subject rather than constantly looking down at your paper.

It is undoubtedly harder to draw a subject when it is moving than when it is still. When I am painting wild animals in Africa, instead

◄ In these figures, sketched while out shopping, movement is suggested by painting one foot shorter than the other, by joining the legs together in a 'V', or inverting the 'V' to imply walking.

▼ **On the Move**
20 x 56 cm (8 x 22 in)
Wet-in-wet is perfect for the backgrounds of moving subjects. It gives the impression of blur, and therefore suggests that the objects in front are moving. Note how the limbs of the animals fade out towards their extremities.

of following the changing movements of one animal I look for another that has taken up a similar position. Herd animals and people in groups repeatedly echo the positions of their peers.

Look for the pattern of the legs, and rather than finish the leg off with the finality of a foot, leave the end of the leg indistinct.

Photographs to the rescue

Since the famous photographs of equine motion taken by Eadweard Muybridge at the end of the nineteenth century the camera has proved to be an invaluable tool when painting movement. With it you can catch the immediacy of moving shapes and transfer them to your paintings. Some actions happen too fast even to sketch; here the camera is invaluable. If you are working from photographs, however, beware making your figures look static within their movement. Still remember to blur a little or leave something slightly unfinished or indistinct. Try to imagine you are actually painting from life and the figure is about to change position. Put pressure on yourself to

work fast so that the brush stroke will retain its energy and spontaneity.

Suggestion of activity

Even still life and flower paintings can benefit from a hint of movement. Shadows move and light dances, petals lift and fall. Letting colours spread wet-in-wet into the background gives the appearance of momentary movement. Thin washes that extend beyond the edges of the objects suggest an adjustment in the parallax of the eye and indicate time passing. If your painting looks too static wet the areas beside hard edges and encourage or drag the colour into the surrounding area to blur the edge.

◀ To paint the swiftly moving horses I loaded the brush with Sepia ink and laid a quick brush stroke for the leading horse. I then added water to my brush and painted the second horse so that the washes blurred slightly together, wet-in-wet. The drawing does not need to be accurate to suggest movement.

Puddle in the King's Road

◀ A Bigger Splash
46 x 66 cm (18 x 26 in)
To create the splash from the puddle I painted masking fluid in energetic brush strokes, following the movement of the water as it careered up from either side and in front of the taxi. This was rubbed off when the painting was dry and touched in with directional brush strokes in places.

Textures and Surfaces

Surface textures are not only great fun to paint but look wonderful in watercolour. To paint every last detail of an intricate texture is extremely absorbing, but it is time consuming, so I am going to suggest a few textural techniques that are quick and easy to do and look very effective.

Sponging

The irregular surface of a natural sea sponge is marvellous for painting speckled textures such as light foliage, granite, gravel, flower centres or sprays of tiny flowers. Mix up plenty of paint to a creamy solution and dab the sponge into the mix. Press the loaded sponge on to the area to be painted to make speckles in a lovely random pattern. Build up the patina with different colours, letting each layer dry before patting on the next.

Salt crystals

An exciting, but slightly unpredictable, texture can be created by sprinkling ground salt crystals into a rich wet wash. The salt

◄ When the background wash is dry green paint is dabbed and patted on to the foliage areas with a sponge. A darker layer is added to create the shadows of the foliage masses. The branches are touched in with a fine brush while the paint is still damp.

◄ The rock forms are loosely differentiated with a shadow blue wash. The granite texture can then be built up with successive layers of sponged colours, keeping the overall tone of the boulders in mind.

◄ **Guardians**
28 x 36 cm (11 x 14 in)
Salt crystals were sprinkled at random into strong wet washes of French Ultramarine, Prussian Blue and Burnt Sienna. When the paint was dry the salt was brushed off the paper with the hand, leaving these lovely patterns in its wake.

absorbs the pigment from the wash and leaves an attractive variety of lichen-like patterns on the paper. Only brush the salt crystals off when completely dry.

Dry-brush

Painting with dry paint or splayed brush hairs is ideal for quickly creating a broken, uneven texture. The end of a brush stroke after it has shed almost all its load will create a dry-brush mark, so exploit this property to create texture.

Waxing

The fact that water and oil do not mix provides opportunities for textural effects that the watercolourist can exploit. One of my favourite techniques is to use an ordinary white wax candle. This is perfect both for suggesting a rough texture and for reserving highlights on textured surfaces.

For details sharpen the end of the candle with a scalpel blade and draw or rub the candle over the highlit area. When you apply paint the waxed area resists the watercolour and a lovely broken edge results, with scattered blobs of colour settling in the tooth of the paper where the wax does not catch. You cannot remove the wax once it is laid, so be certain that you want the waxed area to remain unpainted. I use waxing for texture on rocks, walls, people and foliage.

◄ Wax rubbed over dried paint will reserve areas from the next laid wash. In this sketch wax is rubbed on in several stages beneath successive washes to create an interesting texture and highlights on the surfaces.

▼ **Pebbles on the Beach**
20 x 28 cm (8 x 11 in)
Every technique under the sun was applied to this pebble painting. Salt crystals were tossed into a wet-in-wet variegated wash, the stones picked out wet-on-dry and their textures created with dry-brush, sponging, wax and white gouache.

Al Fresco

Everyday objects are always rewarding to paint and food is no exception. The subject matter comes to life on the paper as the three-dimensional forms become convincing. I arranged the vegetables on the chequered cloth, placing the cauliflower as a backdrop to the smaller forms. To enhance the roundness of the shapes I lit the still-life group from the right.

▶ First stage

Colours

French Ultramarine

Cadmium Red

Indian Yellow

Prussian Blue

Sepia

Yellow Ochre

Crimson Alizarin

First Stage

Having sketched the shapes of the vegetables with an 8B pencil, I half-closed my eyes to ascertain the main lights and darks. I then washed in the areas of shadow with dilute French Ultramarine, using a size 12 sable brush. With this simple tonal wash the forms were already taking shape. I painted masking fluid over the fine trailing roots of the spring onions, so that I could paint freely over them without having to worry about painting round the individual threads.

Second Stage

Next I began to describe the forms with their local colours. I started with a wet wash of Cadmium Red on the tomatoes. Into this I plunged darker colour round the shaded side to enhance the three-dimensional look. I also carried the red into the cloth below, where the redness reflected on the fabric.

While the small orange capsicum was wet I dabbed a touch of red into the Indian Yellow wash, again carrying the colour on to the cloth to show the reflected light. The greens of the pepper, spring onions and cauliflower leaves were made with Prussian Blue and Indian Yellow. For the deliciously dark insides of the mushrooms I used a varying mixture of Sepia, Indian Yellow and Cadmium Red, leaving out thin lines to suggest the gills fanning from the stalk.

Third Stage

Now I could see that the composition and colours were working as a whole I felt confident to work on the three-dimensional form of the individual items. I began by rewetting the centres of the mushrooms with clear water and plunged almost neat Sepia under their rims. A wash of pale Yellow Ochre over the blue on the underside of the back mushroom gave me a suitable warm grey for the slightly dirty-looking white sides.

Then I continued with the tomatoes. I rewetted them from the base, adding Indian Yellow to the top of each tomato and Crimson Alizarin at the bottom.

I now picked a smaller brush, a size 5 sable, for painting around the highlights on the green pepper.

◀ Second stage

As I worked round the whole cauliflower I suggested veins in the leaves by leaving linear gaps between washes. Indian Yellow mixed with Prussian Blue made marvellous non-garish greens.

◀ Third stage

Finished Stage

The chequered lines of the cloth were painted in stripes of French Ultramarine, first in one direction and then, when those were dry, in the other direction. Painting the checks helped to bring out the bulbs of the spring onions.

I stood back from the painting to see how well the vegetables stood out from the paper. I decided the blues of the cloth needed darkening with a little Crimson Alizarin and a dash of Sepia. Then I emphasized the shadows under all the vegetables until they looked good enough to eat!

◀ **Al Fresco**
28 x 38 cm (11 x 15 in)

Making Hay

The shadows were lengthening on a warm summer's day. I wanted to convey the atmosphere of warmth and the golden light. To create distance and a sense of space in the painting I would make the tones of the hills and the back haystacks lighter than the foreground and use the diminishing size of the haystacks to create perspective.

◀ First stage

Colours

Yellow Ochre

Prussian Blue

Crimson Alizarin

Burnt Sienna

First Stage

To give the picture a pervading atmosphere of warmth I decided to underwash the painting with a warm transparent colour that would shine through, and embrace, all the subsequent washes on top. Over a loose pencil sketch I laid an initial wash of Yellow Ochre using a 16 mm (⅝ in) flat sable brush, blending it wet-in-wet at sky level with pale Prussian Blue. I avoided any temptation to 'fill in' any unpainted areas.

Second Stage

The first wash I laid was a pale mauve-grey made from Yellow Ochre, Crimson Alizarin and Prussian Blue. This created the furthermost hill. When this had dried I painted the next hill with wet-in-wet blends in a variegated wash of the same three colours, but slightly darker and much greener. This suggested woodland and fields. The nearest hill was painted in the same way, leaving the fields to dry before painting

in the trees with the same mixture but redder and darker to bring the hill closer.

The standing trees at the edge of the field were painted in a mixture of Crimson Alizarin, Yellow Ochre and Burnt Sienna as the hill wash around them was drying. Some of the wash blended wet-in-wet and some overlapped, giving a combination of hard and soft edges. The trunk of the tree was reserved as tinted paper within the wash.

Third Stage

I painted another underwash over the shapes of the haystacks to enrich and unite them in colour before shaping them with tone. I separated the trees and bushes at the edge of the field by touching darker colour into rewetted corners. Over the foreground of the field I washed Burnt Sienna with a 16 mm (⅝ in) flat brush, leaving the initial ochre wash as the areas of sunshine.

► Third stage

Finished Stage

I now strengthened all the haystacks with Yellow Ochre and a touch of Crimson Alizarin, making the colour stronger on those that were closer and darkening their shaded sides with a purple mixed from Crimson Alizarin and Prussian Blue.

To suggest the stubble in the foreground of the field I made downward strokes with the flat brush that revealed between them the lighter tone of the wash underneath. To create the shadow cast by the foreground haystack I wetted the area above a stubbly grass line and touched some Burnt Sienna and Prussian Blue into the base of the wetted area. The paint spread slightly upward to create a gentle shadow.

◀ **Making Hay While the Sun Shines**
28 x 38 cm (11 x 15 in)

The Texture of Time

Sometimes a detail in a landscape proves more exciting to paint than the landscape scene itself. An old door on the side of an ancient church immediately attracted my interest. Weathered by the elements, wood and stone presented an ideal opportunity to play with four different textural techniques all at once.

▶ First stage

Colours

 Coeruleum

 Burnt Sienna

 Yellow Ochre

 Prussian Blue

 Indigo

 Sepia

Extra materials

Salt crystals

Wax candle

Sponge

◀ Second stage

First Stage

I drew the main lines of the door and stonework, then I wetted the paper with clear water over everything except the centre door panels. Into this I washed Coeruleum, Burnt Sienna, Yellow Ochre and Prussian Blue with a size 10 sable brush and in a random fashion that lent itself to the varied colours of the wall. Immediately, while the paint was still very wet, I dropped ground salt crystals into the wash, again in a random fashion. I dabbed one or two areas with kitchen cloth where rather large pools of coloured water collected. I watched with fascination as the crystals absorbed the pigment from the wash and left glorious patterns as it dried. When totally dry I brushed off the crystals with my hand.

Second Stage

With the sharpened tip of a white household candle I rubbed wax over some of the blocks of stone, leaving out the mortar lines between them. I then washed a mixture of Yellow Ochre and Coeruleum over the wax, which created more texture on the stones, and delineated the stones one from the other with the mortar lines. I washed over the door with dilute Indigo.

Third Stage

To create relief within the brick and stonework I loaded a natural sponge with a greenish creamy mixture and patted it over the corners of stones and areas of indentation.

I darkened the panels of the door with a 16 mm (⅝ in) flat brush and drew shadow lines down the projecting strips of wood with the end of the same brush. Then I darkened the areas under the door and through the little window above the door with a mixture of Indigo and Sepia.

Finished Stage

To suggest wood grain on the door I dipped the flat brush into dryish paint and dragged it over the wooden panels. To paint the spiky unkempt grass I made a dryish mix of Yellow Ochre and Prussian Blue and dragged this colour in layers of upward brush strokes until the foreground blades stood out and appeared to come forward. The addition of the hinges and bolt and some extra delineation between the stones added the final touches.

▶ **The Texture of Time**
38 x 28 cm (15 x 11 in)

Breaking the Waves

Sunsets and sunrises never cease to thrill. The vivid colours provide a wonderful opportunity to use vibrant contrasts. The boy waded into the shallows after his dog, and for an instant they were thrown into stark silhouettes separated by a blinding gulf of light. This dazzling track of reflected sunlight and the contrasting black figures attracted me.

▶ First stage

Colours

 Indian Yellow

 Yellow Ochre

 Cadmium Red

 Prussian Blue

 Crimson Alizarin

 Indigo

First Stage

I mixed up a generous solution of Indian Yellow and then damped the paper all over with clear water, excluding the track of sunlight. With a large mop brush I washed the Indian Yellow all over the damp paper, painting thin strips of yellow across the dry white paper left for the sun's reflection. A little out from the sun's track I added Yellow Ochre to the wet wash, and at the sides I added Cadmium Red. In the top right-hand corner I touched in a swathe of Prussian Blue and Crimson Alizarin. The darker the perimeter of the painting, the lighter the centre will appear.

Second Stage

I waited impatiently for the wash to dry, mixing Prussian Blue, Crimson Alizarin and Cadmium Red together, again in a generous quantity, ready for the dark waves. When it was dry I used a size 10 round sable brush and a 25 mm (1 in) flat brush to paint in the wave shapes with swift directional brush strokes, starting with the tip of the brush and then pressing down the body of the brush to release plenty of pigment into the side of the waves. Where the waves crossed the sun's track I left gaps in the wave washes and then joined them up with ochre and red. I worked fast, pulling out the still wet base of the waves with Prussian Blue and forming it into moving wavelets with a flick of the brush.

When the paint was dry I drew the outline of the boy and his dog with pencil. I painted a guiding orange wash over the silhouettes and reflections in the water so that I would not be tempted just to fill in the shapes with dark colour, but rather paint them as bold overall shapes with the tip and body of the brush.

By using the paint fairly dry I avoided too hard an edge to the silhouettes.

Finished Stage

I mixed Crimson Alizarin and Indigo together for the colour of the silhouettes. I then painted the figures confidently over the orange guide. I carried the colour into the reflections with short sideways brush strokes. I stood back to view, and decided to

make the sun strip more intense by darkening the sides of the painting with Yellow Ochre and Cadmium Red, thus increasing the contrast of light and dark.

▲ Second stage

▼ **Breaking the Waves**
28 x 38 cm (11 x 15 in)

The Adventure Continues

Finally here are just a few reminders to help make your paintings vibrant: keep it simple, contrast light against dark, and do not be tempted to fiddle!

You can learn all the techniques in the world, but the magical two-dimensional world of washes on white paper comes alive because of your passion and your motivation. An inbuilt work ethic often finds it hard to accept that something is worthwhile even if we have not spent too much time on it, but more watercolours are ruined by overworking than by being left alone. If your palette looks more vibrant than your painting you have destroyed watercolour's natural radiance.

It may sound strange to talk of love in terms of painting, but I truly believe it is a vital ingredient in creating vibrant watercolours. By putting yourself, heart and soul, into your painting you can link to the whole of creation.

Relax, have fun, and believe in yourself. Soon you will find that your best paintings are done when you least expect it, when you were relaxed and not trying too hard, when you responded to something you saw that just asked to be painted.

▼ **Le Midi**
25 x 36 cm (10 x 14 in)
This café scene is simplified into a contrast of lights and darks. Few colours are used and little detail is shown, but much is implied.